CW00841055

Kingfisher Books, Grisewood & Dempsey Ltd,
Elsley House, 24-30 Great Titchfield Street,
London W1P 7AD

First published in 1993 by Kingfisher Books
2 4 6 8 10 9 7 5 3

Material in this edition was previously published by
Kingfisher Books in *On the Move: Digger* in 1990.

© Grisewood & Dempsey Ltd 1990, 1993

Series editor: Veronica Pennycook
Series designer: Terry Woodley
Typeset in 3B2
Phototypeset by SPAN
Printed in Great Britain by
BPCC Paulton Books Limited

The Busy Digger

Angela Royston
Illustrated by Philippe Dupasquier

Kingfisher Books

In this book

This book is all about a building machine called a digger. The type of digger in the story is known as a JCB 3CX.

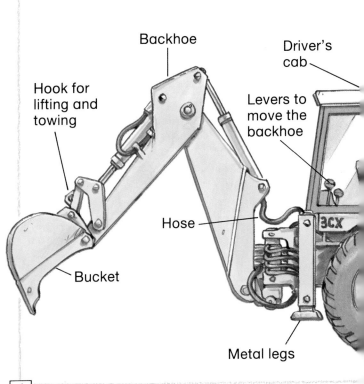

Backhoe

Driver's cab

Hook for lifting and towing

Levers to move the backhoe

Hose

Bucket

Metal legs

3CX

Diggers can do all sorts of jobs. They can lift heavy loads, dig holes, break up rocks and make rough ground smooth.

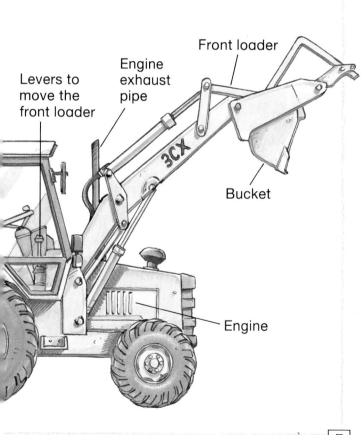

Front loader

Engine exhaust pipe

Levers to move the front loader

3CX

Bucket

Engine

Arriving on site

Early one morning a huge truck
arrives at the building site. It is
carrying a digger. The driver,
Pete, backs his digger off the
truck, then has a quick look
around the site.

Clearing the ground

Pete can see that he will have lots to do, helping to build this new housing estate. Ed, the foreman, shows Pete some bumpy ground that needs to be cleared.

Pete turns his seat around so he is facing the back of the digger.

He lowers the digger's two metal legs. These lift the back wheels off the ground and keep the machine steady. Then he uses the levers that work the backhoe.

He makes the bucket scrape up some rubble. Then he lifts it, and drops it into a dump truck.

Digging foundations

The next morning Pete's job is to dig a trench for the foundations of a house. He fixes a narrow bucket on to the backhoe and scoops out the earth. A dump truck carries the earth away.

When the trench is finished, the concrete mixer arrives. Thick concrete flows down the chute

and into the trench. The concrete
will make a firm surface to build
the foundation walls on.

A forklift truck brings a load of bricks. Once the concrete has set hard, the bricklayers build a low wall on top of it.

When the foundation wall is finished, Pete brings the digger back. This time he uses the front loader to smooth down the earth around the wall. At the same time, he pushes some of the earth right up to the edge of the wall to fill in the trench.

Helping out

One rainy day, Pete is using the digger to clear some ground when Ed runs over to him and shouts, "That truck is stuck in the mud. Can you pull it out?"

The more the truck tries to move, the deeper it sinks.

Pete clips a chain to the hook on the backhoe and fixes it to the front of the truck. He drives the digger forwards and slowly hauls the truck out of the mud.

Laying the drains

Next, Pete has to dig a deep trench to lay drains for the new houses. He fits a wide bucket to the backhoe and scoops out the earth. He dumps it beside the trench so it can be put back later.

Suddenly, the bucket hits a huge lump of rock. "I'll need to break this up," thinks Pete. He takes the bucket off the backhoe and fixes on a giant breaker. The breaker pounds up and down and quickly smashes through the rock.

When the trench is finished, the drainpipes need to be laid. Each pipe is hung from the backhoe and lowered into the trench. Another worker, Jo, tells Pete where to place the pipes. "Left a bit ... now down. That's it."

Break-down

The digger moves on to another job, when suddenly oil spurts from a hose on the backhoe arm. "Oh no!" groans Pete, as the cab window is splattered with oil. He calls out to Ed to ring the mechanics.

Work has to stop until the
mechanics arrive. They put in a
new hose and decide to do a
service while they are there. They
check all the moving parts and the
engine to make sure everything is
working properly and the digger
won't break down again.

Finishing off

The months pass. The houses are nearly all built but the digger is still busy. The bumpy ground behind the houses has to be made into gardens.

Pete uses the digger to clear and

level the ground. Then Jo drives over a dump truck with a load of topsoil and tips it out.

While the dump truck goes for another load, Pete uses the front loader to spread the soil evenly. Soon the gardens are ready.

The next job

The estate is finished at last. Pete and his digger are needed on a new site nearby, and he decides to drive the digger straight there.

Pete fastens a flashing light to the top of his cab to warn other drivers that the digger can only move slowly. Then he loads the spare buckets on to the digger, waves goodbye, and is off to the next job.

Some special words

Breaker   A drill that is fixed to the digger to break up large lumps of rock or concrete.

Foreman   The person in charge of a building site.

Foundations   Walls or pillars built into the ground to be the base of a building.

Housing estate   A group of houses or flats built together.

Mechanic   A person who looks after and mends machinery.

Topsoil   The top layer of earth in which plants grow.

Index